THE DUMBFOUNDING MIND

THE DUMBFOUNDING MIND

RACHEL GELLAR

First Printing, 2025

CONTENTS

CHAPTER 1

Introduction to Stupidity

Defining Stupidity

Stupidity is often perceived as a lack of intelligence or knowledge, yet this simplistic view fails to capture the complexity of the concept. In psychological terms, stupidity can be more accurately described as a failure to utilize available knowledge effectively, particularly in decision-making processes. This distinction highlights that even individuals with high cognitive abilities can exhibit behaviors deemed "stupid" when they succumb to cognitive biases, emotional influences, or social pressures. Understanding stupidity requires a multifaceted approach that incorporates various psychological theories and empirical research.

Cognitive biases play a significant role in the manifestation of what we categorize as stupidity. These biases, such as confirmation bias or the Dunning-Kruger effect, can distort our perception and evaluation of information. For instance, individuals may cling to misinformation or reject factual data that contradict their beliefs, leading to irrational decisions. This cognitive dissonance can be exacerbated in high-pressure situations, particularly for emergency service personnel who must make quick decisions without the luxury of extensive deliberation. Thus, recognizing the influence of cognitive biases is crucial for both understanding and mitigating instances of stupidity in decision-making contexts.

The social dynamics of ignorance further complicate our understanding of stupidity. Individuals often conform to group norms or succumb to peer pressure, which can lead to collectively poor decisions. This phenomenon can be observed in various social settings, from boardrooms to community gatherings. The impact of social dynamics is particularly pronounced when individuals prioritize belonging over critical thinking, resulting in a culture that may foster ignorance rather than enlightenment. Addressing these social influences is essential for encouraging more rational decision-making processes, particularly in environments where collaboration is key.

Education plays a pivotal role in shaping critical thinking skills and, consequently, in combating stupidity. However, the effectiveness of educational systems varies widely, influenced by cultural factors and institutional shortcomings. A curriculum that emphasizes critical thinking, problem-solving, and scientific literacy can equip individuals with the tools necessary to navigate an increasingly complex world. Conversely, an education system that neglects these skills may inadvertently perpetuate cycles of ignorance. The correlation between educational background and the ability to make informed decisions underscores the importance of fostering a culture of learning and inquiry.

Finally, the interplay between emotion and decision-making cannot be overlooked in the discussion of stupidity. Emotional responses often cloud judgment, leading individuals to make choices based on feelings rather than rational analysis. This is particularly relevant in the context of media influence, where sensationalized information can trigger emotional reactions that override logical reasoning. Understanding the neurological underpinnings of intelligence and stupidity, alongside the behavioral economics of decision-making, provides valuable insight into why individuals, regardless of their cognitive capacity, may still engage in seemingly irrational behavior. By exploring these dimensions, we can better comprehend the intricate tapestry of human behavior and the roots of stupidity.

Historical Perspectives on Ignorance

The concept of ignorance has been a focal point in understanding human behavior throughout history, permeating various cultures and intellectual movements. In ancient civilizations, ignorance was often attributed to a lack of knowledge, with philosophers like Socrates emphasizing the importance of self-awareness and the acknowledgment of one's ignorance as the first step toward wisdom. This notion laid the groundwork for later educational philosophies, where critical thinking and questioning became essential tools for enlightenment. The Socratic method, which promotes dialogue and inquiry, illustrates how recognizing ignorance can lead to deeper understanding and informed decision-making, underscoring the historical interplay between knowledge and ignorance.

During the Renaissance, a significant shift occurred as the value of empirical evidence and scientific inquiry gained momentum. The era celebrated humanism and the potential of individual intellect, setting the stage for a more nuanced understanding of ignorance. As thinkers like Galileo and Descartes challenged established norms, they highlighted how ignorance can stem not only from a lack of information but also from cognitive biases that cloud judgment. This period also saw the rise of the scientific method, which sought to mitigate ignorance through systematic observation and experimentation, reflecting an evolving understanding of how ignorance can hinder progress and rational thought.

The Enlightenment further advanced the dialogue surrounding ignorance, framing it as an obstacle to societal progress. Philosophers such as Kant argued that ignorance is not merely a personal flaw but a societal issue that can perpetuate inequality and hinder collective advancement. This perspective opened discussions about the role of education in combating ignorance, emphasizing that informed citizens are essential for a functioning democracy. The social dynamics of ignorance became a critical consideration, revealing how misinformation can flourish within communities, often exacerbated by cultural factors that resist change and challenge established beliefs.

In the contemporary context, the intersection of media and public perception has intensified the challenge of ignorance. The rise of digital information has paradoxically led to both increased access to knowledge and the proliferation of misinformation. Behavioral economics illustrates how emotional responses often drive decision-making, leading individuals to cling to misconceptions even in the face of contradictory evidence. This environment highlights the psychological roots of irrational behavior, where cognitive biases, such as confirmation bias, reinforce ignorance rather than diminish it. Understanding these dynamics is crucial for emergency service personnel and others who must navigate a landscape where misinformation can have serious consequences.

Ultimately, the historical perspectives on ignorance reveal a complex tapestry woven from cultural, educational, and psychological threads. As society continues to grapple with the implications of ignorance, the lessons from the past serve as a reminder of the importance of fostering critical thinking and promoting informed dialogue. By recognizing the multifaceted nature of ignorance and its impact on decision-making, individuals and communities can cultivate an environment conducive to understanding and enlightenment, moving beyond the confines of stupidity towards a more informed and rational future.

CHAPTER 2

The Science of Stupid People

Cognitive Limitations

Cognitive limitations are fundamental to understanding why individuals often engage in seemingly irrational behaviors. These limitations arise from the brain's inherent structure and its processing capabilities, which are not only influenced by biological factors but also shaped by experiential factors such as education and media exposure. Emotions play a pivotal role in decision-making, often overshadowing rational thought. For instance, stress and anxiety can trigger cognitive biases, leading individuals to resort to heuristics that simplify complex decisions but also pave the way for errors in judgment. Recognizing these limitations is essential for emergency service personnel who must make quick, life-or-death decisions under pressure.

Cognitive biases are systematic patterns of deviation from norm or rationality in judgment, and they can significantly distort our perception of reality. These biases often stem from evolutionary adaptations that help humans make quick decisions in uncertain environments. However, in today's fast-paced society, they can lead to poor choices and reinforce ignorance. For example, confirmation bias leads individuals to seek information that supports their preexisting beliefs while ignoring contradictory evidence, which can perpetuate misinformation and misunderstandings, particularly in areas like health and safety. Understanding these biases is crucial for psychology enthusiasts and professionals as they navigate the complexities of human behavior.

The social dynamics of ignorance are also intertwined with cognitive limitations. Groupthink, a phenomenon where the desire for harmony in a decision-making group leads to dysfunctional outcomes, exemplifies how collective cognitive limitations can result in poor decision-making. When individuals prioritize consensus over critical analysis, they often overlook vital information, leading to catastrophic results. This is particularly relevant for emergency service personnel who work in teams and must balance individual input with group cohesion. Awareness of these dynamics can foster better communication and decision-making processes, ultimately improving outcomes in high-stakes situations.

Education is a powerful tool in mitigating cognitive limitations and enhancing critical thinking skills. However, the quality and approach of education significantly impact its effectiveness. Traditional educational models often emphasize rote memorization rather than the development of analytical skills, leaving individuals ill-prepared to confront the complexities of real-world situations. By incorporating critical thinking into curricula, educators can empower individuals to question assumptions and evaluate information critically.

This shift is vital not only for personal development but also for fostering a more informed society that can better navigate the deluge of information prevalent in the media landscape.

Finally, the interplay between cognitive limitations and cultural factors must be acknowledged in discussions of public perception and knowledge. Cultural narratives and societal norms often dictate what is accepted as truth, leading to widespread misconceptions about scientific concepts. This is compounded by media influence, which can amplify these misconceptions through sensationalism or oversimplification. Understanding the neurological underpinnings of intelligence and stupidity helps to unravel these cultural phenomena, revealing the ways in which societal beliefs can distort individual cognition. By addressing these layers, we can begin to foster a more nuanced understanding of human behavior, ultimately improving both personal decision-making and societal outcomes.

The Role of Intelligence in Decision Making

Intelligence plays a crucial role in decision making, influencing not only the choices we make but also the processes by which we evaluate our options. In the realm of psychology, intelligence is often viewed through the lens of cognitive ability, which encompasses reasoning, problem-solving, and the capacity to understand complex ideas. This intellectual framework allows individuals to navigate the myriad decisions they face daily, from mundane choices to significant life-altering ones. However, the interplay between intelligence and decision making is not merely a straightforward correlation; it is intricately affected by various factors including emotional states, social dynamics, and cognitive biases.

Cognitive biases often distort our decision-making processes, leading to choices that may seem irrational or suboptimal. Even individuals with high intelligence can fall prey to these biases, which are systematic patterns of deviation from norm or rationality in judgment. For instance, confirmation bias can lead intelligent individuals to seek out information that supports their pre-existing beliefs while ignoring contradictory evidence. Similarly, the anchoring effect can cause decision-makers to rely heavily on the first piece of information they encounter, regardless of its relevance or accuracy. Understanding these biases is essential for psychology enthusiasts, as it highlights the limitations of intelligence when confronted with the complexities of human cognition.

Emotions also play a significant role in decision making, often overshadowing logical reasoning. Despite the common perception that intelligence equates to rationality, emotional responses can lead even the most astute individuals to make poor choices. The interplay of emotion and intelligence is particularly pertinent in high-stakes environments, such as those faced by emergency service personnel. Here, the pressure of immediate decision making can exacerbate cognitive biases and emotional responses, leading to potentially detrimental outcomes. Acknowledging the emotional undercurrents in decision making allows for a more nuanced understanding of how intelligence operates in practice.

Education is another critical factor that influences the relationship between intelligence and decision making. Higher levels of education typically foster enhanced critical thinking skills, enabling individuals to analyze situations more effectively and make informed choices. However, education alone is not a panacea for poor decision making; it must be accompanied by an awareness of cognitive biases and emotional influences. Moreover, the quality of education matters significantly. In environments where misinformation flourishes, even well-educated individuals can fall into traps of ignorance, demonstrating that intelligence must be complemented by accurate knowledge and critical engagement with information.

Lastly, cultural factors shape our understanding of intelligence and decision making, influencing what is deemed acceptable or rational within different societies. Misconceptions about scientific concepts, for example, can lead to widespread ignorance and poor decision making at a societal level. The media plays a pivotal role in this dynamic, often perpetuating stereotypes or fostering misunderstandings that can skew public perception. By examining the cultural dimensions of intelligence, psychology enthusiasts can better appreciate the complexities involved in decision making, highlighting the need for a holistic approach that recognizes the multifaceted nature of human cognition.

CHAPTER 3

Cognitive Biases and Decision Making

Common Cognitive Biases

Cognitive biases are systematic patterns of deviation from norm or rationality in judgment, highlighting the quirks of human thinking that can lead to poor decision-making. These biases affect everyone, regardless of their level of intelligence or education, illustrating that even the most astute individuals can fall prey to irrational thought processes. For psychology enthusiasts, understanding these cognitive biases is essential for unraveling the complexities of human behavior. Emergency service personnel, who often make split-second decisions under pressure, can particularly benefit from recognizing these biases to improve their response effectiveness and situational awareness.

One of the most prevalent cognitive biases is confirmation bias, where individuals tend to search for, interpret, and remember information that confirms their preexisting beliefs. This bias can lead to the reinforcement of misconceptions, making it difficult for people to change their views even in the face of contradictory evidence. For those engaged in public service or emergency response, awareness of confirmation bias is crucial; it can affect not only their decision-making processes but also their interactions with the communities they serve, as they may inadvertently disregard valuable information that contradicts their assumptions.

Another significant cognitive bias is the anchoring effect, where individuals rely heavily on the first piece of information encountered when making decisions. This can lead to poor judgments, particularly in high-stakes environments where quick assessments are necessary. Emergency service personnel, for instance, may anchor their decisions based on initial observations rather than considering a broader range of evidence. In contrast, understanding the anchoring effect can enhance critical thinking skills, helping individuals avoid making premature conclusions that could have serious consequences.

The Dunning-Kruger effect is yet another cognitive bias that is particularly relevant to discussions of intelligence and decision-making. This phenomenon describes the tendency of those with low ability in a specific area to overestimate their competence, while those with higher ability may underestimate their skills. This bias can lead to a dangerous mix of overconfidence and ignorance, resulting in poor choices and ineffective actions. For emergency responders, recognizing the Dunning-Kruger effect can foster a culture of humility and continuous learning, encouraging personnel to seek further training and expertise.

Lastly, the availability heuristic affects how people assess the likelihood of events based on how easily examples come to mind. This bias can skew perceptions of risk and lead to irrational fears or misplaced priorities. For example, after hearing about a dramatic rescue in the news, an emergency service worker might overestimate the frequency of such incidents, potentially diverting resources or attention away from more probable scenarios. Understanding the availability heuristic can empower individuals to ground their decisions in statistical realities rather than anecdotal evidence, ultimately enhancing their effectiveness in both emergency situations and everyday life.

How Biases Affect Choices

Biases play a crucial role in shaping the choices we make, often leading us away from rational decision-making. Cognitive biases are systematic patterns of deviation from norm or rationality in judgment, and they can significantly impair our ability to evaluate information objectively. In the context of education and critical thinking, individuals may find themselves relying on heuristics—mental shortcuts that simplify decision-making processes. While these shortcuts can be efficient, they often result in oversights and misjudgments, particularly in high-stakes environments like emergency services, where quick, accurate decisions are essential.

One common cognitive bias is confirmation bias, the tendency to search for, interpret, and remember information in a way that confirms one's preexisting beliefs. This bias can lead individuals to ignore contradictory evidence, ultimately reinforcing ignorance. For example, an emergency service personnel may hold a belief about the effectiveness of a particular intervention. If they encounter data suggesting otherwise, their inclination to favor information that aligns with their belief can hinder their ability to adapt to new, potentially life-saving strategies. This not only affects their personal effectiveness but can also impact team dynamics and overall operational success.

Another significant bias is the availability heuristic, which causes individuals to assess the probability of events based on how easily examples come to mind. In a world inundated with media portrayals of crises, emergency service professionals may overestimate the likelihood of rare but dramatic incidents, while underestimating more common, less sensational situations. This skewed perception can lead to misallocation of resources and preparedness efforts, ultimately affecting community safety and response times. The influence of media on public perception further complicates this issue, as sensationalized reporting can distort the reality of risks and emergencies.

Emotional biases also play a pivotal role in decision-making, where feelings can cloud judgment and lead to irrational choices. The role of emotion in decision-making cannot be overstated, as heightened emotional states can trigger impulsive decisions that are later regretted. For instance, stress or fear during high-pressure situations may prompt emergency personnel to make snap judgments without fully considering the consequences. Understanding the neurological underpinnings of such emotional responses can provide valuable insights into how to mitigate their impact, allowing for more reasoned and effective choices in critical moments.

Cultural factors and societal misconceptions further exacerbate the challenges posed by cognitive biases. Shared beliefs and values can shape the way individuals interpret information, often leading to collective biases that hinder critical thinking. For instance, certain cultural narratives may promote a distrust of scientific concepts, leading to widespread misunderstandings that perpetuate ignorance. By fostering an environment that encourages questioning and open discourse, we can challenge these biases and improve decision-making processes. Ultimately, recognizing the myriad ways in which biases affect our choices is essential for cultivating a more informed, rational society capable of addressing complex challenges effectively.

CHAPTER 4

Social Dynamics of Ignorance

Groupthink and Collective Stupidity

Groupthink is a psychological phenomenon that occurs when the desire for harmony and conformity within a group leads to irrational decision-making outcomes. This often results in members suppressing dissenting viewpoints, prioritizing consensus over critical analysis, and ultimately engaging in collective stupidity. In settings where groupthink prevails, individuals may abandon their personal beliefs and critical thinking skills, contributing to decisions that are not only poorly conceived but potentially harmful. This subchapter will explore the mechanisms of groupthink, its psychological roots, and the implications for various social contexts, particularly in emergency services where lives are at stake.

One of the primary psychological underpinnings of groupthink lies in cognitive biases, which skew perception and judgment. Members of a group may succumb to the illusion of invulnerability, believing their team is immune to failure. This false sense of security can lead to overconfidence in decisions, as group members dismiss potential risks or negative outcomes. Additionally, the pressure to maintain group cohesion can stifle dissenting opinions, creating an environment where questioning the status quo is discouraged. The result is a collective mindset that values agreement over rigorous evaluation, fostering an ecosystem ripe for irrational choices.

The social dynamics of ignorance contribute significantly to groupthink. In many situations, individuals may defer to perceived authority figures within the group, allowing these leaders to dominate discussions and influence decisions without challenge. This deference can create a feedback loop, reinforcing the group's shared misconceptions and preventing critical discourse. In emergency service scenarios, where quick decisions are essential, the tendency to rely on group consensus can lead to rapid, yet flawed, courses of action. Understanding these dynamics is crucial for fostering environments where critical thinking is encouraged and valued, thereby improving the quality of decisions made under pressure.

Education plays a vital role in countering the effects of groupthink and enhancing critical thinking skills. Implementing curricula that emphasize analytical reasoning, problem-solving, and the evaluation of evidence can empower individuals to resist the allure of conformity. By cultivating a questioning culture, educational institutions can prepare individuals to engage effectively in group settings, challenging assumptions and advocating for informed decision-making. This shift not only enhances personal cognitive abilities but also equips communities and organizations to confront collective stupidity head-on, making more informed choices that reflect a deeper understanding of complex issues.

Lastly, the influence of media on public perception cannot be understated in the context of groupthink. Media narratives often shape the collective consciousness, sometimes perpetuating misinformation or oversimplifications of complex topics. When groups consume similar media, they may unwittingly align their beliefs and decisions with these narratives, fostering a homogenization of thought. This phenomenon can lead to the reinforcement of collective stupidity, as individuals become less likely to seek out diverse perspectives or challenge prevailing narratives. By recognizing the interplay between media influence and group dynamics, psychology enthusiasts, humor seekers, and emergency service personnel can develop strategies to mitigate the potential pitfalls of groupthink, promoting a culture of informed decision-making.

The Influence of Social Media on Knowledge

The rise of social media has fundamentally altered the landscape of information dissemination, creating a dual-edged sword in the realm of knowledge acquisition. With the click of a button, vast amounts of data can be shared, reshaping how individuals engage with information. While this democratization of knowledge can empower users to access diverse perspectives, it simultaneously fosters a breeding ground for misinformation. The rapid spread of false information can lead to cognitive biases, where individuals confirm their pre-existing beliefs rather than challenge them, often at the expense of critical thinking. This phenomenon highlights the importance of understanding social media's influence on collective knowledge and the psychological implications it entails.

Cognitive biases play a significant role in how users interpret information on social media platforms. Confirmation bias, for instance, leads individuals to seek out information that aligns with their beliefs, while ignoring contradictory evidence. This is particularly evident in discussions surrounding controversial topics, where echo chambers reinforce existing misconceptions. As users engage with content that resonates with their viewpoints, they may become increasingly resistant to changing their opinions, perpetuating ignorance. The algorithms that govern social media platforms often exacerbate this issue by curating content that is likely to attract engagement, further entrenching users in their cognitive biases.

The social dynamics of ignorance are also amplified in online environments. Groups of individuals can rally around shared beliefs, creating a sense of community that is often predicated on misinformation. This phenomenon can be traced back to the psychological need for belonging, which can override the desire for accurate information. As people increasingly rely on social validation from their peers rather than empirical evidence, the propagation of flawed knowledge becomes more pronounced. Emergency service personnel, for instance, may encounter situations where public misunderstandings, fueled by social media narratives, lead to irrational behaviors during crises, complicating response efforts.

Education plays a critical role in mitigating the negative effects of social media on knowledge. Promoting media literacy and critical thinking skills can empower individuals to navigate the complexities of online information. By fostering an environment where questioning and skepticism are encouraged, educators can equip students with the tools necessary to discern credible sources from misleading ones. Moreover, understanding the emotional underpinnings of decision-making can help individuals recognize how feelings can cloud judgment, especially when engaging with emotionally charged social media content. This awareness is crucial for cultivating a more informed public.

In conclusion, the influence of social media on knowledge is a multifaceted issue that intertwines various psychological and social factors. The interplay between cognitive biases, social dynamics, and emotional influences highlights the challenges individuals face in seeking accurate information. As the landscape of knowledge continues to evolve with the proliferation of social media, it becomes imperative for psychology enthusiasts, emergency service personnel, and the wider public to develop a critical awareness of these dynamics. By acknowledging the psychological roots of irrational behavior and fostering a culture of informed decision-making, society can take meaningful steps toward countering the tide of ignorance in the digital age.

CHAPTER 5

Psychological Roots of Irrational Behavior

Fear and Anxiety in Decision Making

Fear and anxiety are potent emotions that can dramatically affect decision-making processes. When faced with uncertainty, individuals often experience heightened stress levels, which can cloud judgment and lead to irrational choices. This phenomenon is particularly evident in high-pressure environments, such as emergency services, where split-second decisions can mean the difference between life and death. Understanding how fear and anxiety influence decision-making can provide valuable insights into both individual behavior and broader social dynamics.

Cognitive biases play a crucial role in how fear and anxiety manifest in decision-making. The availability heuristic, for instance, can cause individuals to overestimate the likelihood of negative outcomes based on recent experiences or media portrayals. When fear is a dominant emotion, individuals may gravitate towards the most sensationalized stories, believing that their chances of encountering similar situations are higher than they statistically are. This skewed perception can exacerbate anxiety, leading to a cycle of poor decision-making that is rooted in an irrational assessment of risks.

Moreover, the social dynamics of ignorance can amplify fear and anxiety in group settings. In environments where misinformation is prevalent, individuals may rely on the opinions of others rather than their own critical thinking skills. This reliance can create a feedback loop where collective anxiety drives group decisions that are often irrational. For emergency service personnel, this can result in a reluctance to act decisively in critical moments, as the fear of making the "wrong" choice becomes paralyzing. Understanding these social dynamics is essential for fostering environments where informed decision-making can thrive.

The impact of education on critical thinking cannot be overstated in the context of fear and anxiety. A well-rounded education encourages individuals to question their assumptions and analyze situations from multiple perspectives. When faced with fear-inducing scenarios, educated individuals may be better equipped to recognize their emotional responses and apply rational thought to their decisions. Conversely, those with limited exposure to critical thinking strategies may struggle to navigate fear and anxiety, leading to choices that are more reflective of emotional turmoil than logical reasoning.

Finally, the role of emotion in decision-making cannot be underestimated, particularly in the context of fear and anxiety. Neuroscience has shown that emotional responses are often processed in the amygdala, a region of the brain associated with threat detection. When fear signals are strong, they can hijack the rational thinking processes of the prefrontal cortex, resulting in decisions that may seem illogical in hindsight. This interplay between emotion and cognition highlights the importance of developing emotional intelligence to recognize and manage fear and anxiety effectively, paving the way for more rational decision-making amidst the complexities of life.

The Dunning-Kruger Effect

The Dunning-Kruger Effect is a cognitive bias that highlights a peculiar paradox: those who possess limited knowledge or skill in a particular domain often overestimate their competence, while individuals with a more profound understanding tend to underestimate their abilities. This phenomenon can be observed across various fields, from emergency response to everyday decision-making, where a lack of expertise can lead to overconfidence. The implications of the Dunning-Kruger Effect extend beyond individual psychology, influencing group dynamics, decision-making processes, and even public policy. Understanding this effect is essential for psychology enthusiasts and professionals alike, as it sheds light on the complexities of human cognition and the pitfalls of self-assessment.

In practical terms, the Dunning-Kruger Effect manifests in numerous scenarios. For example, emergency service personnel might encounter individuals who, despite minimal training, believe they can effectively manage crisis situations. This overconfidence can lead to dangerous outcomes, not only for the individual but also for those they aim to assist. Recognizing the effect allows these professionals to approach situations with a more nuanced perspective, fostering an environment in which expertise is valued and sought after, rather than dismissed. This awareness can enhance teamwork and improve overall outcomes in high-stakes situations where accurate assessment of skill is crucial.

Moreover, the Dunning-Kruger Effect has significant implications for societal dynamics and public discourse. In an age where information is readily available, individuals often find themselves misinformed yet confident in their opinions. This is particularly evident in discussions surrounding science and public policy. The tendency to misjudge one's understanding can contribute to the spread of misinformation, as individuals with limited knowledge may dismiss expert opinions in favor of their own unfounded beliefs. This phenomenon not only affects individual decision-making but also shapes societal attitudes towards critical issues, from health to climate change, highlighting the need for effective communication and education.

The roots of the Dunning-Kruger Effect can be traced to several psychological factors, including metacognition—the awareness of one's own cognitive processes. Those lacking in knowledge may not possess the metacognitive skills necessary to accurately evaluate their competence, leading to inflated self-assessments. This deficiency creates a cycle where ignorance perpetuates itself, fostering an environment where false confidence reigns. In contrast, individuals with greater expertise are often more aware of the complexities and uncertainties within their field, which can lead to a more tempered view of their abilities. This insight underscores the importance of fostering critical thinking skills and encouraging a culture of lifelong learning.

Finally, the Dunning-Kruger Effect serves as a reminder of the broader cultural factors that influence misconceptions and ignorance. Social dynamics, media influence, and educational systems all play critical roles in shaping public perception and knowledge. By addressing the factors that contribute to cognitive biases like the Dunning-Kruger Effect, stakeholders in education and public policy can work towards promoting a more informed and critical populace. This requires not only enhancing individual understanding but also creating systems that reward humility and the pursuit of knowledge, ultimately leading to better decision-making and a more rational society.

CHAPTER 6

The Impact of Education on Critical Thinking

Educational Systems and Their Shortcomings

Educational systems are often hailed as the primary vehicle for cultivating intelligence and critical thinking, yet they frequently fall short of their aspirational goals. One major shortcoming lies in the rigid curricula that prioritize rote memorization over genuine understanding. This approach can stifle creativity and critical thinking, leading students to regurgitate information without grasping its underlying concepts. The emphasis on standardized testing further exacerbates this issue, as educators feel pressured to "teach to the test" instead of fostering a deeper intellectual curiosity. Consequently, students may graduate with impressive grades but lacking the ability to apply their knowledge in real-world scenarios, a phenomenon that often leads to poor decision-making in adulthood.

Moreover, the educational systems often neglect the emotional and social dimensions of learning. Emotional intelligence plays a crucial role in how individuals process information and make decisions. However, traditional education models tend to prioritize cognitive skills over emotional development, which can result in a disconnection between knowledge and practical application. This gap is particularly evident in emergency service personnel who must make rapid, often life-or-death decisions. Without the tools to understand and manage their emotions, even the most educated individuals can succumb to irrational behavior, illustrating how a lack of comprehensive educational approaches can lead to detrimental outcomes.

Cultural factors also contribute to the shortcomings of educational systems. Different cultural backgrounds influence how knowledge is perceived and valued, which can create misunderstandings and misconceptions. For instance, in societies where questioning authority is discouraged, students may feel compelled to accept information without critical analysis. This cultural context can breed ignorance, as individuals fail to engage with scientific concepts or challenge common misconceptions. As a result, the educational system may inadvertently perpetuate ignorance rather than combat it, thus hindering progress in critical thinking and informed decision-making.

Furthermore, the media's influence on public perception complicates the educational landscape. The pervasive nature of misinformation in the digital age can warp the knowledge acquired through formal education. Many individuals turn to media sources for information, but these often prioritize sensationalism over factual accuracy. This misalignment can create a disconnect between academic knowledge and public understanding, resulting in poor decision-making driven by emotional responses rather than rational thought. Consequently, education systems must adapt to address the growing impact of media on how knowledge is consumed and understood among the populace.

Ultimately, the shortcomings of educational systems underscore the need for a holistic approach to learning that integrates cognitive, emotional, and social dimensions. By recognizing the importance of critical thinking, emotional intelligence, and cultural contexts, educators can better prepare students for the complexities of real-world decision-making. In doing so, they can help mitigate the effects of cognitive biases and irrational behavior, fostering a generation that is not only knowledgeable but also capable of navigating the challenges that lie ahead. This comprehensive understanding of education's role in shaping thought processes is essential for addressing the broader issues of ignorance and stupidity in society.

Promoting Critical Thinking Skills

Promoting critical thinking skills is essential for navigating the complex landscape of information in today's society. As individuals engage with diverse media and interact within various social contexts, the ability to analyze, evaluate, and synthesize information becomes increasingly vital. Critical thinking empowers individuals to assess the validity of claims, recognize cognitive biases, and make informed decisions. This capacity is particularly crucial for psychology enthusiasts and emergency service personnel, who often operate in high-stakes environments where rapid decision-making can significantly impact outcomes.

In the realm of education, fostering critical thinking skills is paramount. Traditional educational models frequently emphasize rote memorization and standardized testing, which can stifle analytical thinking. Innovative teaching strategies, such as inquiry-based learning and problem-solving exercises, can encourage students to engage actively with content. By prioritizing questions over answers, educators can cultivate an environment where curiosity thrives, enabling learners to explore concepts deeply and develop their reasoning abilities. This approach not only enhances individual cognitive skills but can also lead to a more informed populace that is less susceptible to misinformation.

The influence of media on public perception and knowledge cannot be understated. In an age where information is abundant, the challenge lies in discerning credible sources from those that propagate falsehoods. Critical thinking skills equip individuals to navigate this media landscape effectively. By evaluating the reliability of sources and understanding the potential biases inherent in various forms of media, individuals can resist the allure of sensationalism and misinformation. This skill set becomes especially crucial for emergency service personnel, who often rely on accurate information to make life-saving decisions in uncertain situations.

Cognitive biases play a significant role in decision-making processes, often leading individuals to make irrational choices. By promoting critical thinking, individuals can become more aware of these biases, such as confirmation bias or anchoring bias, which can cloud judgment. Understanding the psychological roots of irrational behavior allows individuals to reflect on their thought processes and make more deliberate choices. This self-awareness is particularly beneficial in high-pressure environments where emotional responses can lead to poor decision-making, underscoring the importance of critical thinking in reducing the impact of such biases.

Finally, cultural factors can significantly shape common misconceptions and misunderstandings of scientific concepts. Promoting critical thinking skills involves not only individual cognitive development but also addressing the broader societal influences that contribute to ignorance. By encouraging open dialogue and fostering a culture of questioning, communities can challenge prevailing misconceptions and enhance collective understanding. This cultural shift is essential for creating a society that values knowledge and critical inquiry, ultimately leading to better decision-making and a more informed citizenry.

CHAPTER 7

Media Influence on Public Perception and Knowledge

The Role of Media in Shaping Beliefs

The media plays a crucial role in shaping beliefs and perceptions, acting as both a mirror and a mold for societal attitudes. From news outlets to social media platforms, the information disseminated influences how individuals interpret the world around them. This influence is particularly pronounced in contexts where cognitive biases come into play, such as confirmation bias, where individuals favor information that confirms their preexisting beliefs. When media sources present information selectively or sensationally, they can reinforce existing misconceptions and lead to an environment where ignorance flourishes, thereby impacting decision-making processes.

Cognitive biases are not just individual quirks; they are often exacerbated by media portrayal of events. For example, the framing of news stories can dictate the emotional response of the audience, leading to irrational beliefs and behaviors. When a news outlet focuses on violent crimes while downplaying positive community actions, it can skew public perception, creating a belief that violence is more prevalent than it actually is. This skewed perception can lead to fear-driven decisions and policies that do not reflect the reality of statistical data. The role of media, therefore, extends beyond mere reporting; it actively shapes the narrative that influences societal norms and individual choices.

Moreover, the rapid dissemination of information through digital platforms has transformed the landscape of belief formation. Social media algorithms prioritize engagement over accuracy, leading to the spread of misinformation and reinforcing echo chambers. Individuals are often exposed to a limited range of viewpoints, which can further entrench their beliefs and diminish their critical thinking skills. This phenomenon is especially concerning for emergency service personnel, who rely on accurate information for decision-making in high-stakes situations. Poorly informed beliefs can lead to suboptimal responses in crises, highlighting the real-world implications of media influence.

Education plays a pivotal role in counteracting the detrimental effects of media on belief formation. Critical thinking skills are essential for navigating the overwhelming amount of information available today. By fostering an educational environment that encourages questioning and skepticism, individuals can become more discerning consumers of media. Understanding the psychological roots of irrational behavior can also aid in recognizing when emotional responses overshadow logical reasoning. This knowledge is vital for both psychology enthusiasts and professionals who aim to understand the complexities of human behavior in the context of media influence.

Ultimately, the interplay between media and belief formation underscores the importance of fostering media literacy. As societies become increasingly reliant on digital platforms for information, the need for individuals to critically evaluate sources and content has never been more pressing. Engaging with diverse perspectives and questioning prevailing narratives can mitigate the effects of cognitive biases and enhance decision-making processes. By recognizing the media's role in shaping beliefs, we can work towards a more informed and rational society, minimizing the impact of ignorance and fostering a culture of understanding and critical analysis.

Misinformation and Its Consequences

Misinformation, defined as false or misleading information disseminated without malicious intent, has become a pervasive issue in modern society. Its rapid spread is fueled by social media, which allows for instantaneous sharing of content, regardless of its accuracy. This phenomenon reflects a broader cultural challenge where individuals often prioritize sensationalism and emotional resonance over factual accuracy. The consequences of misinformation are profound, affecting not only individual decision-making but also public perception and societal dynamics. Understanding these effects is crucial for psychology enthusiasts, emergency service personnel, and anyone invested in fostering informed communities.

One of the most significant consequences of misinformation is its impact on decision-making processes. Cognitive biases, such as confirmation bias and the Dunning-Kruger effect, play a crucial role in how individuals interpret information. When people encounter misinformation that aligns with their pre-existing beliefs, they are more likely to accept it as truth without critical evaluation. This can lead to a cycle of ignorance where erroneous beliefs become entrenched, making individuals resistant to new information. Emergency service personnel, who often rely on accurate data for life-or-death decisions, can find themselves undermined by public misconceptions, which complicate their response efforts.

The social dynamics of ignorance are further exacerbated by groupthink and the influence of social networks. When misinformation circulates within a community, it can create echo chambers where dissenting voices are drowned out. As individuals seek validation from their peers, they might ignore credible sources in favor of popular opinion. This collective endorsement of falsehoods can lead to widespread misunderstandings, particularly during crises when accurate information is critical. The psychological roots of irrational behavior can be traced back to these social influences, highlighting how group identity can override rational thought.

Education plays a vital role in combating misinformation and enhancing critical thinking skills. Individuals equipped with the tools to assess the reliability of sources and differentiate between fact and opinion are better positioned to navigate the complexities of information in the digital age. However, the effectiveness of education in promoting critical thinking depends on its ability to engage students actively. Innovative approaches that encourage curiosity and skepticism can empower individuals to challenge misinformation rather than passively accept it. This is particularly important in fostering a culture that values informed decision-making and resilience against the onslaught of misleading information.

Finally, the interplay between media influence and public perception cannot be overlooked. Media outlets, driven by ratings and engagement, often prioritize sensational stories that capture attention, even at the expense of accuracy. This can lead to a distorted understanding of reality among the public, where emotional responses overshadow rational analysis. The role of emotion in decision-making is a critical factor in this dynamic, as fear or outrage can cloud judgment and lead to impulsive choices. By recognizing the mechanisms behind misinformation and its consequences, individuals can better navigate the complexities of modern information landscapes, fostering not only personal growth but also collective resilience against the pitfalls of ignorance.

CHAPTER 8

Behavioral Economics: Understanding Poor Choices

Decision Fatigue and Overwhelm

Decision fatigue is a psychological phenomenon that occurs when the quality of decisions deteriorates after a long session of decision-making. In an age characterized by an overwhelming amount of choices—from the mundane, such as what to eat for breakfast, to the significant, such as career paths or relationships—individuals often find themselves paralyzed or resorting to poor choices. This cognitive overload can lead to a state of overwhelm, where the mind becomes exhausted from the relentless need to analyze options, weigh pros and cons, and predict potential outcomes. Understanding decision fatigue is crucial, especially for emergency service personnel who must make quick, effective decisions under pressure.

The roots of decision fatigue are deeply embedded in cognitive psychology. Each choice we make requires cognitive resources, and as these resources diminish, so does our ability to make sound judgments. Research indicates that after a day filled with decisions, people tend to opt for the easiest route rather than the most beneficial one. This can manifest in various ways, such as opting for unhealthy food choices or procrastinating on important tasks. For those in high-stakes professions, like emergency responders, the implications can be dire, as even minor lapses in decision-making can result in significant consequences.

Moreover, the concept of cognitive biases amplifies the effects of decision fatigue. Cognitive biases are systematic patterns of deviation from norm or rationality in judgment. They can skew perceptions and lead to irrational decisions, especially when an individual is mentally fatigued. For instance, the availability heuristic can cause a person to overestimate the likelihood of an event based on recent experiences or media coverage, leading them to make choices not grounded in statistical reality. In contexts where accurate risk assessment is paramount, such as in emergency services, understanding these biases becomes essential for improving decision-making processes.

Emotional factors further complicate the landscape of decision fatigue. Stress, anxiety, and emotional turmoil can cloud judgment, pushing individuals towards impulsive decisions that may not align with their best interests. The interplay between emotion and cognition is critical in understanding why people make seemingly foolish choices, particularly under pressure. This chaotic blend of overwhelming choices, cognitive exhaustion, and emotional strain can foster an environment ripe for irrational behavior, making it imperative to develop strategies to combat decision fatigue.

Educational initiatives that focus on critical thinking and decision-making skills can help mitigate the impacts of decision fatigue. By fostering an understanding of cognitive biases, emotional regulation, and effective decision-making strategies, individuals can be better equipped to navigate the complexities of their choices. For those engaged in high-stakes environments, such as emergency service personnel, training that emphasizes rapid assessment and decision-making under pressure can significantly enhance their performance and reduce the likelihood of poor choices stemming from fatigue and overwhelm. By addressing the psychological roots of irrational behavior, we can cultivate a more informed and thoughtful populace, better prepared to confront the challenges of decision-making in an increasingly complex world.

The Cost of Poor Decision Making

The cost of poor decision-making is multifaceted, impacting individuals and society in profound ways. At the individual level, the consequences of bad choices often manifest as financial losses, damaged relationships, and missed opportunities. For instance, someone might impulsively invest in a dubious scheme, only to find themselves in a precarious financial situation. In the realm of personal relationships, decisions rooted in emotional reactions can lead to conflicts and estrangement, underscoring how irrational behavior can quickly spiral into significant personal costs. Understanding the psychological roots of these decisions can illuminate why individuals fail to weigh the potential outcomes critically, often ignoring evidence in favor of emotion-laden choices.

Moreover, the ramifications of poor decision-making extend beyond individual lives to societal implications. When leaders or organizations make flawed choices, the effects can reverberate through communities and economies. For example, public health decisions based on incomplete data can lead to widespread misinformation and ineffective responses to crises, as seen during various health emergencies. This highlights the critical role of cognitive biases in decision-making processes, where misjudgments stem from overconfidence, confirmation bias, or groupthink. Such errors can lead to systemic issues that require extensive resources and time to rectify, emphasizing that the stakes of poor decision-making are not just personal but societal.

Education plays a pivotal role in shaping critical thinking and decision-making skills. Those with a robust educational background are often better equipped to analyze information, recognize cognitive biases, and make informed choices. Conversely, a lack of emphasis on critical thinking in educational systems can perpetuate cycles of ignorance and poor decision-making. This gap can create a population vulnerable to manipulation, especially in an age where media influence is pervasive. The dissemination of misleading information can skew public perception, leading to collective poor choices that affect health, safety, and policy decisions on a larger scale.

The emotional component of decision-making also warrants attention, as our feelings can heavily influence our choices. Often, individuals rely on gut feelings or emotional responses rather than rational thought, leading to decisions that may appear illogical in hindsight. This phenomenon is well-documented in behavioral economics, where the interplay of emotion and reason is explored. Understanding the neurology of how emotions affect decision-making can provide insights into why intelligent individuals sometimes make seemingly foolish choices, demonstrating that intelligence does not always equate to sound judgment.

Cultural factors further complicate the landscape of decision-making. Common misconceptions rooted in cultural narratives can shape how individuals approach choices, sometimes leading them astray. For example, certain cultural beliefs may discourage questioning authority or embracing uncertainty, fostering environments where poor decisions can thrive. By exploring these dynamics, we can better grasp how social and cultural influences contribute to irrational behavior. Ultimately, recognizing the cost of poor decision-making, both on an individual and societal level, emphasizes the need for improved critical thinking skills and a more nuanced understanding of the psychological factors at play in our everyday choices.

CHAPTER 9

The Role of Emotion in Stupid Decisions

Emotional Triggers and Impulsive Choices

Emotional triggers play a significant role in the impulsive choices individuals make, often leading to decisions that may appear irrational or unwise. This phenomenon is particularly relevant for psychology enthusiasts and emergency service personnel, who frequently encounter situations where emotions run high. When faced with stress or strong feelings, such as fear or excitement, the brain often bypasses logical reasoning in favor of immediate emotional responses. This can result in decisions that, while satisfying in the moment, may have long-term negative consequences. Understanding these emotional triggers can provide insight into why seemingly intelligent individuals sometimes act against their better judgment.

The human brain is wired to respond to emotional stimuli, often prioritizing feelings over rational thought. This is evident in the context of cognitive biases, where emotions can distort perception and influence decision-making. For instance, the availability heuristic leads individuals to make judgments based on recent emotional experiences rather than objective data. In emergency situations, the urgency of the moment can exacerbate this effect, compelling first responders to make snap decisions that may not align with standard protocols. Recognizing these biases is crucial for improving critical thinking skills, especially in high-pressure environments.

Moreover, social dynamics play a significant role in shaping our emotional responses and subsequent choices. Groupthink, for instance, can amplify emotional triggers, leading individuals to conform to group decisions that may not be rational. This social pressure can further cloud judgment, making it challenging to break away from collective impulses. When individuals prioritize acceptance or fear of conflict over sound reasoning, the potential for poor choices increases. This is a critical area of focus for those interested in the behavioral economics of decision-making, where understanding the interplay between emotion and social influence can lead to better outcomes.

Education also plays a vital role in equipping individuals to handle emotional triggers effectively. By fostering critical thinking and emotional intelligence, educational systems can prepare individuals to navigate their feelings and make more informed choices. Programs that emphasize the integration of emotional awareness with logical reasoning can help mitigate the effects of impulsive decisions. This is particularly important in fields such as emergency services, where the ability to remain calm and collected can directly impact the outcome of a situation.

Finally, the media's influence on public perception further complicates the relationship between emotion and decision-making. Sensationalized reporting can heighten emotional responses, leading to misguided beliefs and actions. When individuals rely on emotionally charged media narratives, they may become susceptible to misinformation and irrational behavior. This creates a cycle where emotional triggers, coupled with cognitive biases and social dynamics, result in decisions that defy logic. Understanding these intricate connections is essential for psychology enthusiasts and professionals alike, as it sheds light on the underlying mechanisms of human behavior and the often perplexing nature of stupidity.

The Intersection of Emotion and Rationality

In exploring the intersection of emotion and rationality, we uncover how deeply intertwined these two elements are in shaping human behavior. Emotion often serves as a powerful driving force behind decisions, frequently overshadowing logical reasoning. For psychology enthusiasts, understanding this interplay is crucial, as it reveals the fundamental mechanisms that lead to both sound judgment and poor decision-making. Emergency service personnel, for instance, may experience heightened emotional responses in crisis situations, which can impede their ability to think clearly and act rationally. This dynamic is pivotal in high-stakes environments where split-second decisions can have significant consequences.

Cognitive biases, rooted in our emotional responses, play a significant role in how we perceive and interpret information. When emotions run high, individuals are more likely to succumb to biases such as confirmation bias, where they favor information that aligns with their feelings, while dismissing contradictory evidence. This phenomenon is especially relevant in understanding the social dynamics of ignorance, as public perception can often be swayed by emotionally charged narratives rather than factual accuracy. Such biases can create a feedback loop, reinforcing misconceptions and leading to widespread misinformation.

The psychological roots of irrational behavior are often found in the emotional landscapes of individuals. When faced with uncertainty or fear, people may default to irrational choices as a means of coping with their feelings. For instance, the phenomenon of loss aversion illustrates how the fear of losing something can lead to decisions that prioritize short-term emotional relief over long-term rational benefits. This tendency is particularly evident in behavioral economics, where understanding why individuals make poor choices can illuminate the emotional underpinnings that drive those decisions.

Education plays a pivotal role in shaping critical thinking skills, yet its effectiveness can be compromised by the emotional responses that arise during discussions of controversial topics. The impact of education on decision-making is profound, as it can equip individuals with tools to navigate their emotional reactions more effectively. However, the challenge lies in fostering environments where rational discourse can occur, free from the divisive influence of emotions. This is particularly vital in media contexts, where sensationalism can exacerbate emotional responses, leading to misinformed public opinion.

Cultural factors also contribute to the misunderstandings of scientific concepts and the emotional narratives that often overshadow reasoned debate. Different cultures may have varying levels of acceptance for scientific reasoning, influenced by historical beliefs and emotional attachments to those beliefs. By examining these cultural dynamics, we can better understand how emotions can distort perceptions of knowledge and facts. Recognizing the delicate balance between emotion and rationality can empower individuals, including psychology enthusiasts and emergency service personnel, to navigate the complexities of decision-making in a more informed and effective manner.

CHAPTER 10

Neurology of Intelligence and Stupidity

Brain Structure and Function

The brain is an intricate organ that orchestrates a myriad of functions essential for our everyday activities. Understanding its structure is crucial to grasp how various cognitive processes unfold, particularly those related to decision-making and irrational behavior. At its core, the brain comprises several key regions, each associated with different functions. The cerebral cortex, responsible for higher-order processes such as reasoning, problem-solving, and critical thinking, plays a pivotal role in how we evaluate information and make decisions. The interplay between the cerebral cortex and other brain areas, such as the limbic system, which governs emotions, often leads to the irrational choices we observe in everyday life.

Cognitive biases, which are systematic patterns of deviation from norm or rationality in judgment, are often rooted in the brain's structural organization. These biases can lead individuals to make poor choices, influenced by emotions rather than logical reasoning. For instance, the amygdala, which processes emotions, can overpower the analytical capabilities of the prefrontal cortex. This imbalance can result in decisions fueled by fear or anxiety, leading to behaviors that may seem irrational or "stupid" in hindsight. For psychology enthusiasts, dissecting these biases provides insight into the cognitive shortcuts our brains take, often with detrimental effects on our decision-making processes.

The social dynamics of ignorance are also influenced by brain structure and function. The brain's reward system, which releases dopamine in response to positive reinforcement, affects how we engage with information. When individuals receive social validation for certain beliefs, even if they are factually incorrect, the reward system reinforces these beliefs, leading to a cycle of ignorance. This dynamic is especially relevant in understanding how misinformation spreads and persists within communities. Emergency service personnel, who often rely on critical thinking in high-stakes situations, may find this knowledge particularly valuable as it emphasizes the importance of accurate information in decision-making.

Moreover, the impact of education on critical thinking cannot be understated. Educational environments that encourage inquiry and skepticism can promote healthier cognitive functioning and reduce susceptibility to biases. Neuroscientific research indicates that the brain can adapt and reorganize itself through learning, a phenomenon known as neuroplasticity. This adaptability highlights the potential for improving critical thinking skills and reducing irrational behaviors through targeted educational interventions. Engaging with this knowledge can empower both individuals and communities to combat the forces of ignorance that often lead to poor choices.

Finally, the neurological underpinnings of intelligence and stupidity reveal much about the human condition. Cultural factors play a significant role in shaping our understanding of intelligence, with varying definitions and expectations across different societies. The brain's structure is not static; it evolves based on experiences, education, and environmental influences. This evolution is crucial for understanding how misconceptions about science and rational thought can spread and become entrenched. By examining these aspects, we can better understand the complexities of human behavior, especially how emotions, cultural contexts, and cognitive frameworks contribute to the phenomenon of stupidity.

The Neuroscience of Learning and Memory

The intricate relationship between neuroscience, learning, and memory forms a foundational pillar in understanding human behavior, particularly when exploring the roots of irrationality and ignorance. Neuroscience reveals how our brain structures, such as the hippocampus and prefrontal cortex, play crucial roles in processing, storing, and retrieving information. The hippocampus is essential for forming new memories, while the prefrontal cortex governs higher-level cognitive functions, including decision-making and critical thinking. These areas work in tandem to help us navigate our environments, make informed choices, and learn from experiences. However, when these systems are compromised, whether by stress, fatigue, or cognitive biases, the potential for poor decision-making and the perpetuation of ignorance increases.

Learning is not merely a passive absorption of information; it is an active, dynamic process influenced by emotions, context, and social interactions. Emotional responses can enhance or hinder our ability to learn. For instance, anxiety can impair memory retrieval, while positive emotions can facilitate retention and recall. This emotional undercurrent is particularly relevant when examining the psychology of stupidity. When individuals experience strong emotions, their decision-making processes can become clouded, leading to irrational choices that defy logical reasoning. Such behaviors often stem from an interplay of cognitive biases, where personal beliefs and societal influences distort our understanding of information.

Moreover, the social dynamics of ignorance cannot be overlooked. Humans are inherently social beings, and our learning often occurs within group contexts. The phenomenon known as social learning suggests that individuals frequently mimic the behaviors and beliefs of those around them, which can perpetuate misconceptions and irrational beliefs. This collective ignorance can be further exacerbated by media influence, as sensationalized or biased information shapes public perception and knowledge. The neurological basis for this is linked to mirror neurons, which play a role in empathy and imitation, thereby influencing our learning processes in social environments.

Cognitive biases also significantly impact our decision-making capabilities, leading to poor choices that defy rational thought. These biases, such as confirmation bias and the Dunning-Kruger effect, illustrate how our perceptions can skew our understanding of reality. For instance, individuals with limited knowledge in a subject may overestimate their expertise, resulting in misguided confidence. This disconnect between perceived and actual knowledge highlights the need for critical thinking and education as tools to counteract these biases. Educational methodologies that encourage questioning and critical analysis can help mitigate the effects of cognitive distortions, fostering a more informed populace.

Finally, understanding the neurological underpinnings of intelligence and stupidity requires an exploration of cultural factors and their influence on misconceptions. Different cultures prioritize various forms of knowledge, which can shape how individuals interpret information and make decisions. This cultural lens affects not only personal beliefs but also collective societal norms regarding science and education. By recognizing these influences, emergency service personnel and psychology enthusiasts alike can better appreciate the complexities of human cognition. Ultimately, fostering an awareness of the neuroscience behind learning and memory can empower individuals to challenge their assumptions, make better decisions, and navigate the often convoluted landscape of information in an increasingly complex world.

CHAPTER 11

Cultural Factors in Common Misconceptions

Cultural Narratives and Ignorance

Cultural narratives play a pivotal role in shaping perceptions and understanding, often leading to widespread ignorance. These narratives are deeply embedded in societal norms and values, influencing how individuals process information and make decisions. They can perpetuate misconceptions and biases that cloud judgment, resulting in irrational behavior. When cultural narratives distort reality, they create a fertile ground for ignorance to thrive, making it imperative to dissect these stories to understand their psychological impact on decision-making and social dynamics.

The social dynamics of ignorance are intricately linked to cultural narratives, as individuals often rely on the collective wisdom of their communities. This reliance can foster an environment where misinformation proliferates, as people may choose to accept widely held beliefs without scrutiny. Cognitive biases, such as confirmation bias, lead individuals to favor information that aligns with their existing beliefs while dismissing contradictory evidence. This phenomenon highlights the tension between individual reasoning and collective narratives, underscoring how cultural influences can inhibit critical thinking and perpetuate a cycle of ignorance.

Education serves as a crucial counterbalance to cultural narratives that promote ignorance. By fostering critical thinking skills and encouraging inquiry, educational systems can challenge established narratives and illuminate misconceptions. However, the effectiveness of education in combating ignorance often depends on its ability to engage students emotionally and intellectually. When learners connect personally with the material, they are more likely to question prevailing narratives and develop a deeper understanding of complex issues. This emotional engagement is vital in breaking down barriers created by cultural narratives that can inhibit rational thought.

The media also plays a significant role in shaping cultural narratives and influencing public perception. With the rise of social media and the 24-hour news cycle, the dissemination of information has become instantaneous and often unfiltered. This environment can amplify ignorance, as sensationalized narratives capture attention while more nuanced, accurate information is overlooked. The interplay between media narratives and public knowledge underscores the importance of media literacy as a skill necessary for discerning factual information from misleading representations. Understanding how media influences cultural narratives can empower individuals to critically evaluate the information they consume.

Ultimately, addressing cultural narratives and their role in fostering ignorance requires a multifaceted approach. It necessitates an understanding of the psychological roots of irrational behavior, the impact of emotional responses on decision-making, and the cultural factors that contribute to common misconceptions. By examining these elements, psychology enthusiasts, humor seekers, and emergency service personnel can gain insights into the dynamics of ignorance within their fields. Embracing this knowledge not only enhances personal understanding but also equips individuals to challenge ignorance in their communities, paving the way for more informed decision-making and healthier social interactions.

The Impact of Tradition on Knowledge

Tradition plays a significant role in shaping our understanding of knowledge, often acting as both a vessel for wisdom and a barrier to critical thinking. Societies worldwide have developed customs, beliefs, and practices passed down through generations, creating a framework through which individuals interpret their realities. While these traditions can foster a sense of identity and community, they may also perpetuate misconceptions and stifle the pursuit of knowledge. In the context of psychology, it is crucial to explore how these longstanding practices influence cognitive biases, decision-making processes, and the overall quality of knowledge that individuals possess.

One of the most profound effects of tradition on knowledge is its ability to create cognitive shortcuts, or heuristics, that guide decision-making. People often rely on established norms and values to make choices, which can lead to both efficiency and error. For instance, the tendency to adhere to traditional beliefs may result in the dismissal of new information that conflicts with those beliefs, a phenomenon known as confirmation bias. This bias not only limits the capacity for critical thinking but also reinforces ignorance, as individuals may become resistant to exploring alternative viewpoints or evidence that challenges their traditional understanding.

Moreover, the influence of tradition extends to the educational system, where curricula may reflect historical biases and cultural narratives that prioritize certain perspectives over others. This can have lasting effects on critical thinking and the ability to engage with scientific concepts. When educational frameworks are rooted in tradition, they may inadvertently promote a static view of knowledge, discouraging students from questioning established ideas or exploring innovative approaches. As a result, the development of critical thinking skills is often hampered, leaving individuals ill-equipped to navigate complex issues or make informed decisions in an increasingly dynamic world.

The relationship between tradition and media also plays a crucial role in shaping public perception and knowledge. Media outlets often reinforce traditional narratives, which can perpetuate stereotypes and misconceptions. This is particularly evident in how certain social dynamics and cultural factors are portrayed, leading to a skewed understanding of reality. Emergency service personnel, for instance, may find that traditional media representations of emergencies influence public expectations and responses, complicating their decision-making processes. Acknowledging the impact of media and tradition on knowledge is essential for fostering a more nuanced understanding of the world.

In conclusion, while tradition can enrich our lives and provide a sense of belonging, it is imperative to recognize its potential to hinder the pursuit of knowledge. The interplay between tradition, cognitive biases, education, and media influences the way individuals understand and engage with the world around them. For psychology enthusiasts and humor seekers alike, examining these dynamics offers valuable insights into the roots of irrational behavior and the common misconceptions that persist in society. By fostering an awareness of how tradition shapes knowledge, we can encourage critical thinking and empower individuals to make more informed choices, ultimately enhancing our collective understanding of intelligence and stupidity.

CHAPTER 12

Misunderstandings of Scientific Concepts

The Importance of Scientific Literacy

Scientific literacy is an essential skill that empowers individuals to navigate the complexities of modern life. In an age where information is abundant yet often misleading, the ability to critically evaluate scientific claims is more crucial than ever. For psychology enthusiasts and emergency service personnel alike, understanding scientific principles can aid in recognizing and countering cognitive biases that often lead to poor decision-making. By fostering a mindset grounded in scientific reasoning, individuals can improve their judgment and enhance their ability to respond effectively in high-pressure situations.

The roots of irrational behavior often lie in a lack of scientific understanding, leading to misconceptions that perpetuate ignorance. Psychological research highlights how cognitive biases—systematic patterns of deviation from norm or rationality—affect our perceptions and choices. When individuals are ill-equipped to discern valid scientific information from pseudoscience, they become susceptible to making decisions based on flawed reasoning. This is particularly relevant in emergency services, where quick, informed decisions can mean the difference between life and death. A solid foundation in scientific literacy can help professionals in these fields make evidence-based decisions, ultimately improving outcomes for those they serve.

Education plays a pivotal role in cultivating critical thinking skills, which are vital for scientific literacy. However, the current educational landscape often fails to adequately address this need, resulting in a populace that may struggle to engage with complex scientific topics. A curriculum that emphasizes inquiry, skepticism, and the scientific method can equip individuals with the tools necessary to evaluate evidence and question assumptions. By prioritizing scientific literacy in education, we can foster a generation that is better prepared to confront the challenges of misinformation and to advocate for rational discourse in public debates.

Media influence compounds the challenge of achieving widespread scientific literacy. The rise of sensationalism and the prevalence of clickbait have distorted public perception and understanding of scientific issues. This distortion can lead to widespread misconceptions, as individuals are often drawn to emotionally charged narratives rather than factual reporting. In this environment, it is vital for individuals to develop the skills to critically analyze media content. By becoming discerning consumers of information, people can mitigate the risks associated with misinformation and better understand the scientific concepts that underpin societal issues.

Cultural factors also play a significant role in shaping our understanding of science and the prevalence of ignorance. Societal norms and values can dictate what is accepted as knowledge, often leading to the perpetuation of common misconceptions. Engaging with diverse cultural perspectives in the context of scientific literacy can illuminate how various groups interpret scientific information. By recognizing and addressing these cultural influences, we can work towards a more informed society capable of making rational, evidence-based decisions. Ultimately, enhancing scientific literacy is not just about understanding facts; it is about fostering a culture of inquiry and rationality that benefits everyone.

Addressing Misconceptions in Society

Addressing misconceptions in society is a crucial endeavor, particularly in an age where information is as accessible as it is abundant. Many individuals harbor erroneous beliefs that can lead to poor decision-making and reinforce cognitive biases. These misconceptions often arise from a lack of understanding or misinterpretation of scientific concepts, which can be exacerbated by media portrayals and cultural narratives. The psychological roots of such misunderstandings can be traced back to various cognitive biases, including confirmation bias, where individuals favor information that aligns with their pre-existing beliefs, and the Dunning-Kruger effect, which leads those with limited knowledge to overestimate their understanding.

The role of education in mitigating these misconceptions cannot be overstated. Educational systems that emphasize critical thinking and scientific literacy are essential in empowering individuals to discern valid information from misinformation. This is especially relevant in emergency service personnel training, where quick and accurate decision-making can mean the difference between life and death. By fostering an environment that encourages questioning and exploration, we can equip individuals with the tools necessary to navigate complex situations without falling prey to irrational behavior stemming from misconceptions.

Media influence is another significant factor that shapes public perception and knowledge. Sensationalized reporting and the proliferation of faux news can distort understanding and perpetuate misconceptions. The emotional impact of such media can further cloud judgment, leading to decisions based on fear or misinformation rather than factual evidence. It is vital for psychology enthusiasts and humor seekers alike to recognize the power of media narratives and to engage with information critically, seeking out reliable sources and employing fact-checking techniques to counteract the spread of falsehoods.

Cultural factors also play a pivotal role in the persistence of misconceptions. Different societies may prioritize certain beliefs and practices that are not grounded in scientific understanding, which can lead to widespread acceptance of erroneous ideas. This cultural lens through which information is viewed can create barriers to critical thinking and open discussion. Understanding these dynamics can help in crafting more effective communication strategies that resonate with diverse audiences, ultimately fostering a more informed society.

In conclusion, addressing misconceptions in society requires a multifaceted approach that integrates education, media literacy, and an understanding of cultural influences. By recognizing the psychological underpinnings of irrational behavior and the impact of cognitive biases, individuals can become better equipped to challenge their own beliefs and those of others. This collective effort can create a ripple effect that enhances decision-making processes across various domains, contributing to a more rational and informed public discourse.

CHAPTER 13

Moving Forward from Stupidity

Strategies for Improving Understanding

In addressing the challenge of improving understanding, it is essential to recognize the interplay between cognitive biases and decision-making processes. Psychology enthusiasts can benefit from examining how various cognitive traps, such as confirmation bias or the Dunning-Kruger effect, contribute to the persistence of ignorance. By fostering awareness of these biases, individuals can cultivate critical thinking skills that allow them to scrutinize their beliefs and decisions more effectively. Workshops and discussions that focus on recognizing these cognitive distortions can serve as practical tools in this endeavor, equipping participants with the knowledge necessary to navigate complex information landscapes.

Education plays a pivotal role in enhancing critical thinking abilities. Implementing curricula that prioritize analytical skills, problem-solving, and the scientific method can lay the groundwork for more informed decision-making. For emergency service personnel, training that emphasizes evidence-based practices and situational analysis can be particularly beneficial. Engaging in case studies and simulations encourages learners to apply theoretical knowledge to real-world scenarios, ultimately empowering them to make sound judgments under pressure. By incorporating these educational strategies, individuals can develop a more nuanced understanding of the factors that influence behavior, thus improving their overall decision-making process.

The impact of media on public perception and knowledge cannot be overstated. In an era dominated by information overload, it is crucial to instill media literacy as a fundamental skill. Understanding how media frames information can lead to more discerning consumption of news and social narratives. Psychology enthusiasts and humor seekers alike can benefit from critical evaluations of media content, recognizing the techniques used to sway opinion or perpetuate misconceptions. This awareness can foster a more skeptical approach toward sensationalist narratives, allowing individuals to seek out reliable sources and scrutinize the validity of the information presented.

The emotional underpinnings of decision-making also warrant attention when discussing strategies for improving understanding. Emotions often drive irrational behavior, leading individuals to make choices that contradict logical reasoning. By understanding the role of emotions in decision-making, individuals can learn to pause and reflect before acting on impulse. Techniques such as mindfulness and emotional regulation can be integrated into training programs for both psychology enthusiasts and emergency personnel, enhancing their ability to assess situations calmly and make more rational decisions. This emotional intelligence can serve as a powerful counterbalance to the instinctual responses that often lead to poor choices.

Lastly, addressing cultural factors that contribute to common misconceptions is vital for enhancing collective understanding. Different cultural backgrounds shape the way individuals perceive and interpret information, often leading to misunderstandings of scientific concepts. Engaging in open dialogues that celebrate diversity while challenging erroneous beliefs can foster an environment where knowledge is shared and misconceptions are clarified. By promoting cultural competence and sensitivity in discussions surrounding science and rational thought, we can create a more informed community that values critical thinking over ignorance. Through these strategies, we can bridge the gap between knowledge and understanding, ultimately combating the stigma of stupidity in our society.

The Future of Education and Knowledge Dissemination

The future of education and knowledge dissemination is poised for a transformative shift, driven by advancements in technology and a deeper understanding of cognitive biases. As we grapple with the complexities of human behavior, educational approaches must evolve to address the roots of irrationality and ignorance. The integration of cognitive psychology into educational frameworks can enhance critical thinking skills and promote a more nuanced understanding of decision-making processes. By focusing on how emotions and biases influence our choices, we can create curricula that not only inform but also empower learners to navigate an increasingly complex world.

One significant aspect of this evolution is the growing emphasis on personalized learning experiences. Traditional educational models often adopt a one-size-fits-all approach, which can overlook the diverse cognitive styles and emotional responses of individuals. By leveraging data analytics and adaptive learning technologies, educators can tailor content to meet the specific needs of students. This customization allows learners to engage with material that resonates with their unique experiences, thereby fostering a deeper understanding of complex subjects such as behavioral economics and the social dynamics of ignorance.

Moreover, the role of media in shaping public perception and knowledge cannot be understated. As information becomes more accessible, the challenge lies in discerning credible sources from misinformation. Education systems must equip individuals with the tools to critically evaluate media messages and understand the psychological underpinnings of their own biases. By incorporating media literacy into the curriculum, we can cultivate a generation that is not only informed but also skeptical of unverified claims, thereby reducing the prevalence of common misconceptions.

The integration of technology into education also creates opportunities for collaborative learning experiences that transcend geographical boundaries. Online platforms can facilitate discussions among diverse groups, enriching the learning process through exposure to varied perspectives. This social dynamic can be particularly beneficial in understanding cultural factors that contribute to irrational behavior and misconceptions. By engaging in dialogue with peers from different backgrounds, learners can challenge their own biases and develop a more comprehensive understanding of complex issues.

Finally, as we look to the future, it is essential to recognize the importance of emotional intelligence in education. Understanding the emotional roots of irrational behavior can inform teaching strategies that promote resilience, empathy, and critical reflection. By fostering environments where learners feel safe to question and explore their beliefs, educators can cultivate a culture of inquiry that encourages deeper engagement with knowledge. As we advance into this new era of education, the goal should be to create not just informed individuals, but critical thinkers who can navigate the intricacies of human behavior and contribute positively to society.

www.ingramcontent.com/pod-product-compliance
Lightning Source LLC
LaVergne TN
LVHW100331210926
848480LV00003B/1304
* 9 7 9 8 3 4 8 2 4 3 7 2 2 *